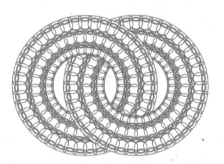

# BOY

# BOY

## A SEQUENCE OF POEMS

### TRACY YOUNGBLOM

CAVANKERRY PRESS

CavanKerry Press Ltd.
Fort Lee, New Jersey
www.cavankerrypress.org

Publisher's Cataloging-in-Publication Data
provided by Five Rainbows Cataloging Services
Names: Youngblom, Tracy, author.
Title: Boy / Tracy Youngblom.
Description: Fort Lee, NJ : CavanKerry Press, 2023.
Identifiers: ISBN 978-1-933880-99-0 (paperback)
Subjects: LCSH: Grief. | Children—Death. | Motherhood. | Fathers and daughters. |
    Spirituality. | American poetry—21st century. | BISAC: POETRY / Subjects
    & Themes / Death, Grief, Loss. | POETRY / Subjects & Themes / Family. |
    POETRY / Women Authors.
Classification: LCC PS3625.O96 B69 2023 (print) | DDC 811/.6—dc23.

Cover artwork: Broken Mirror courtesy of Shelby Edwards/Stocksy United;
    Silhouette of a young boy courtesy of simpleinsomnia/Flickr.com
Cover and interior text design by Ryan Scheife, Mayfly Design
First Edition 2023, Printed in the United States of America

CAVANKERRY
PRESS

Made possible by funds from the
New Jersey State Council on the Arts, a partner
agency of the National Endowment for the Arts.

CavanKerry Press is grateful for the support it receives from the
New Jersey State Council on the Arts.
In addition, CavanKerry Press gratefully acknowledges generous emergency support
received during the COVID-19 pandemic from the following funders:

The Academy of American Poets

Community of Literary Magazines and Presses

The Mellon Foundation

National Book Foundation

New Jersey Arts and Culture Recovery Fund

New Jersey Council for the Humanities

New Jersey Economic Development Authority

Northern New Jersey Community Foundation

The Poetry Foundation

US Small Business Administration

**Also by Tracy Youngblom**

*Driving to Heaven* (2010)
*Growing Big* (2013)
*One Bird a Day* (2018)

In memoriam
Timothy Bruce Sjolie
1968–1972

# CONTENTS

## 3: BARELY ANY WORDS

## 4: SUDDENLY INCOMPREHENSIBLE

## 5: NO LEAVING

## 6: SHAPELESS AS THE DARK

## 7: CRIES OF SUCH PITCH

# PROLOGUE

Imagine a mirror dropped
and shattered, a certain beauty

in the fragmented, mosaiced
wreckage: it appears arranged,

purposeful. Artfully confusing.
That is illusion. Nothing fits

together, there's no surface, just
images lifted and hurled against

each other—that's how it is
with fractured memory, the past.

Not to mention the bad luck
it is to enter—it's like a crime

syndicate: even casual involvement
will cost you your innocence.

I didn't break the mirror.
I wouldn't choose to rummage.

My face is hidden even from
myself. You can cut yourself open

or see something that is not there,
trying to retrieve or repair.

Maybe a cobbled version of that boy's
life will emerge if I crawl long

enough, mustering the faith
of the doubtful.

# 1 : THE OTHER TRUE STORY

**i.**

Before his heartbeat, it was Christmas:
presents scattered like building blocks,

then a new carpet of wrapping paper.
Our father looked down from

his fuzzy height and said, *Time for bed,*
but he meant *beer,* and chased us off

with no story except the one
his recklessness was reciting

to my mother. If he had seen us even
a moment—his small wavering flames—

breathed his story of power on us—
we would have been extinguished.

Instead, he climbed on my mother
to narrate, implanting the earliest

version of my brother, those two
joined cells locked in their struggle

to become the same sound in two
volumes: *thump THUMP, thump*

*THUMP, thump THUMP.*

ii.

When my melon mother finally expelled

her guts, it was a son, but she wouldn't
believe it. *Don't lie to me,* she yelled

at the doctor. His bloody body proof

enough to vow: she had everything
she wanted now, missing

the cosmic joke. She forgot

that when God peopled the earth—
according to his desire—

he wasn't satisfied. That's why

he tried to kill us off. And why,
even when he's not the agent

of our deaths, he already is.

iii.

The moon, that big innocent eye,
was wide open the night

he was born. It saw the beefy boy
arrive face up. A year later, its image

lit up the blue face of a TV, blurred
by the strange motion of men

wading through air so thin
they nearly lost control in it.

It was a slim dipping moon
that night, a winking moon—

knowing. It knew that
in just three years it would cast

its full light down on the boy
who'd knocked his head so hard

he'd never get up. *That* evening
the moon would shine

so brightly, it could blind.

**iv.**

Up close, everything is different.

We are watching TV
at the neighbors'. Our father

is talking to the grown-ups.
Our mother is gone—*away*—

but sends gifts: nubbly brown
and orange potholders she wove,

a glittery clown picture for my brother,
just under a year. She is not sick,

just needs a *rest*. Tonight, we don't
think of her, but gape at the moon's

real face on the screen—how dull,
how dusty—with the boys next door,

happy to eat dinner here
rather than at home where our father

burns peas, steams potatoes to mush,
where he waves his long arms, spoon

in hand, proclaiming his hero—Hitler—
man who almost took over the world,

where we see him close up for the first

time—what he loves.

## v.

A boy in a field is just a boy,
unless he's lost and wandering.

Then the field becomes his conflict,
and he becomes the character

who must resolve it. (God seems
to have abandoned him, which we

identify as foreshadowing.) But enter us,
makeshift neighborhood gang.

We spread out like posses in all
the good old Westerns, to snare him

in our human trap. He will not
escape our fears (we thrust aside

witchgrass at each step). We resolve
to corral him home, ignore that catch

under our shirts, knowledge of the alternate
ending (we peer at the ground

for a flash of blue jacket or blood).
He will be restored, scrubbed with hugs

and by our mother in the bath.
We will bear with us this memory

and this one: the potential
for disaster, the other true story.

vi.

Breeze draws everything upward: Sheets
on the line twirl over and over, become a sheath.

Embers from last night's small fire rise
in the air, dark birds spinning. Petals

from the flowering crab litter the grass—
then, lifted by wind, they begin their wild

ascension. My eyes follow them as if the sky
could absorb all their silken curves

or reveal the answers to my troubled questions.

**vii.**

Stairs: a way to enter
or exit.

Rise and tread:
two known parts of stairs,

as in *up we come, down we go,*
opposing motions.

But: opposite of rise is fall.
Opposite of tread? Not tread . . .

wait? stall? sink? fall?
Must be fall, the action

and the season so similar:
the heedless tumbling toward

approaching darkness.

**viii.**

Late June: our world is giddy
with light and heat. We visit

our new cousin, wrinkled boy
wrapped head to foot, just his plump

face visible, take turns cradling
him, one elbow propped on

the rocker's armrest. Our brother
is too young to take a turn:

*A baby can't hold a baby.* He breathes in
the new boy's face:

*Ain't he cute?* We rock, we hum,
we hold onto him, keep him safe,

our brother standing watch,
separate in his awe.

**ix.**

Such portent at your birth:

youngest boy in a family
of girls—wished for, loved—

too much? We sisters meant

business, bore down to help
you, love that wanted to keep you

always small. It would not be.

Or it would. That day,
you were just trying to visit

the dog, only other boy around. You were

sick—heartsick?—missed your grip
and spun, grasping at nothing—not railing,

but sudden air—tumbled down,

took in a patchy last view: open
doorway, sunlit kitchen. That's the story

I invent: your final glance something

to carry with you. That's not all
I imagine: those bumps—one step

at a time—the fatal one—and your

breaths at the last—not gasps—
a steady slowing, the body as it wades

in water, the water like hands stroking

the skin—so death would have been
gentle. Dear God, here's futility:

thinking like this: pretending
I am talking to you and not

expecting an answer.

# 2: SLIDE BECOMES FALL

**x.**

Summer: it's wild, no holds barred.
You can't stop or slow it:

not its light, not its grass that grows
in an afternoon, not its pollen

scattered so thickly on breeze
you can taste it, not morning

glories with their puckered
old lady faces, not lake-splash

or sprinklers or children
who leap into waves without fear,

come up spitting water
like fountains. It speeds by

and you speed with it, sliding
along the long days as if

sliding down a pile of slippery
oats. If slide becomes fall, don't

expect summer to notice—too full
of its own burgeoning. Summer

is like that—single-minded
in its desire to be nearly

out of control.

**xi.**

In 1972, everyone has a finished basement
except us. We are behind: we have 2 x 4 studs,

no sheetrock, cement floors, unadorned

wooden stairs. Between each set, a patch
of open air that we girls glimpsed

as we tumbled down—those spaces

a respite. At the bottom, we stood
up, undid our bumps:

walked back up, ate dinner as usual,

washed dishes afterwards.
Afterwards, he was not like us.

Doctors said he would never.

*If they sawed off the top of his head?*
No. *If they did nothing?*

(They did.) Other people choosing,

moving past us into the future—
we were used to that.

**xii.**

Middle sister, I had time to grow
at home with invisibility: I rode

the yellow stuffed horse
to my own vision of forever

while my sisters and brother
stacked blocks with our father,

toppling their own worlds
with one swipe of a hand.

Later, wading through a field
of neighbors after my brother fell,

no one saw me. I hadn't been there
to see the fall, the fallen boy.

No way to undo that absence
or belong. My first grief

secondhand, borrowed. Suspect.

**xiii.**

Late June heat. I play catch

with someone, maybe field fly balls—
something. I know I have ridden

my bike here, crossed a highway.

Then a strange car pulls up. A woman—
her glasses triangular vises

that squeeze her eyes—gets out.

*Your brother hurt himself and had to go to
the hospital.* I huff without hurry

to my bike. Pedal home. Encounter

a swarm of people, my irritation
swallowed by something larger. As I make

my way, elbow by elbow, I try

to forget my longing to be part
of the breath-holding crowd who saw

his limp body and drilled down for hope.

**xiv.**

We think a lot. But we can't think
*dead.* So, we wait. The living room alive

with motion: everyone who knew him
to breathe is here. Then: the next

morning. Then: my parents appear
in a strange car, get out, walk up

the front hill together. Our father
may be drunk, he is holding her

elbows, bent over her bent head.
Sudden truth flares, a thought

that sickens: our brother has died.
Otherwise, he would not carry her

by the elbows up the hill to a house
where he no longer lives.

Maybe—our minds leap—he will come
home—yes—if he did not mean to,

they wouldn't walk like that:
back together. We know if we wait

until they get to the door
to cry, it will be so.

# 3 : BARELY ANY WORDS

**xv.**

To get really good at something,
you practice: Grandpa and great

aunts and uncles in their coffins taught
us to mourn until we got it

right: futile crying, heads
full of wrongheaded wishes.

At my grandpa's funeral, I
believed my tears drawing lines

on his made-up cheek
could bring him back. But I

was older now. My brother
was closed off, his face hidden.

In movies the left-behind throw
themselves over the caskets,

hysterical. Not me. All that practice
paid off: each tear served

to the God who thought it up:
burying a boy whose coffin

was only as long as my arm
span. *I know your game,*

I prayed. *I've been cheated.*

**xvi.**

Memories are like this: beach
full of sandpiles blown flat.

Funerals also: fields of collapsed
senses, a child's house of blocks

scattered. You were closed off
because your gauze-wrapped head

would have kept everyone
from prayer. Early July: breeze

blowing in from open doors flanking
the altar. My father—yours—

hunched over in a pew, head
resting on one hand, snot

and unintelligible words draining
from him. Almost infectious:

no one bothered to touch him.
The priest had a catch

in his voice, trying to attach
meaning to your death, while

I cried into a plaid shirt.
Later, hands fumbled us

toward dry ham sandwiches
that clogged our throats. Even

birdsong tacked to air scratched
our ears. It hurt to hear

and not to: your anticipated,
absent voice, the echo of that final

song the singing priest chose because
he couldn't know any better:

*To everything (turn, turn, turn)*
*there is a season (turn, turn, turn)*

*and a time to every purpose*
            *under heaven.*

**xvii.**

Silence of aftermath:
emptiness: chair

with no boy, undented
pillow on the made bed,

that bear I found
in the closet, sealed

in a plastic bag, its round
dark puddle eyes, red

felt mouth curdled
by words—as we all—

when we tried to speak
of it—what was.

**xviii.**

*It sucks to be pure and predictable,*
said the moon. *Can't I be dark*
*and offensive sometimes?*

*What the fuck,* said God,
*you have to give the people*
*what they want.*
*For example, I created*
*the world. They believe I will keep*
*bringing new life—babies,*
*hydrangeas, rainbows*
*(just a modest trick of light).*
*So I bring it.*

*But they don't really notice*
*me,* the moon whined.
*I'm cliché, background,*
*white noise. They look, but*
*they don't see.*

Then the moon had
a revelation:
*You take away life too,*
*you bastard. Yes,* smiled
God, *because I make it.*

*Go ahead, tell the sun*
*you want to make your own*
*light. Then be as full of dark*
*promise as you please.*

**xix.**

Even when it appears, the truth
can be ignored—one can close

one's eyes to it, see what
is not there—transform it

into one's own image: each label
promising love, liquid

swishing in the glass tempting
as hips, tongue receiving

its first taste—a kiss—natural
and fulfilling. One becomes

a living inversion: stagger appears
as graceful walk, fury

a version of love, slurred
words electric speech. We do not

blame the moon, which appears
to brighten the sky by itself.

We know better. It is the same
with our father, as incapable

of generating his own light
as we are of looking away.

**xx.**

We could tell there was snot dripping
down and words dripping out

of his loose, lousy mouth
when he called later to beg

for our love. The kitchen all hard
surfaces: linoleum and stiff

dishrags and enamel. It was too
much: that *wah-wah* pedal of need.

We scurried, scrubbing to a gleam,
while the receiver trembled, attached

to the palm of my mother's outstretched
hand, a strobe light making our flurried

movements cool. We grooved on our way
of coping: ignore everything. His voice

bounced around the hollow room
where we had once sat bowed

in prayer. We kept vigil, warding off
any temptation to need him again, eyed

the receiver back into its cradle. Refused
to weep. Never spoke of it again.

**xxi.**

We didn't know him except
he was our father, now sober

enough to hold a job. We trudged
to work with him on his weekends

at *Pizza Papa,* stretched and slung
dough, suffered the rain of flour

until we became ghosts or angels.
At 2 am, we answered late-night

good-byes of the regulars
with small silent waves: *Good night.*

*You girls look so much like*
*your father. You should be proud*

*of him.* We drove home in
the dark, hunched in the back

seat. Up front, his head far above
us, his face lit up by passing

streetlights. We rode in his
shadow. Looked only to him,

just as he needed us to.

**xxii.**

His objects are hidden all over
the house: bear in the closet

sealed in plastic, cowboy hat
in my mother's headboard

cubby, the plaid shorts and yellow
shirt he wore that last Father's Day—

stashed somewhere. We have nothing:
no money, barely any words. We keep

his name to ourselves. But we secretly
unwrap that dumb bear to rub

our hands over its worn fur.

# 4: SUDDENLY INCOMPREHENSIBLE

**xxiii.**

The funeral has passed, we
are intact: our babysitter comes

as usual. Nothing is usual.
On the table, a stack of cards

splits open to reveal a stack of money—
fives and tens riffling in the air.

Gone that stout, blue-eyed boy
with his plaid shorts and cowlick—

but this: my little sister exclaiming,
*We're rich!* We laugh because

it's not true, because the truth
is so plain: the world pulses

outside the window: apple blossoms
and robins and a yard

that needs mowing. All this.
Whether or not we close

our eyes to it.

## xxiv.

Jesus and Lazarus came back
from the dead and each week

we stood at my brother's grave
and prayed. The ground never

heaved, our feet never moved.
Words on the stone were wrought,

carved for all time. As we left,
we paused at the gravesites

of other children buried in his row:
infant daughter Reichert,

whose family we didn't know,
many dead babies of the Meisters,

whom we did. They lived, each of them,
only days. Our brother had lived

almost four years. How lucky
we should have felt.

**xxv.**

Look—it's the moon
in the morning, hanging

low in the sky where
it doesn't belong.

Sometimes, too, at night,
when all that shows

is a sliver of lip, the lit mouth
of a shrouded face,

the moon isn't itself
either. A body,

disembodied. Almost
unnatural.

**xxvi.**

That first Christmas: presents
from my grandmother: white
vinyl go-go boots, mittens, albums
(*The Partridge Family* for me).

Mother had said, *Don't expect presents.*
She gave us a package anyway—
Ping-Pong balls, a net—the table
waiting at home. Such luxury

stole our breath. Dinner was finished:
roast beef, rich gravy,
the mashed rutabagas I loved.
No one would play Ping-Pong
with me on the kitchen table. I stomped
my feet, carried on—all alone in
the kitchen—so embarrassing:
I was nine.

Mother led me away to talk. I didn't
want to talk, I wanted _____.

She gripped my shoulders, spoke
words that struck like
a slap from which I recoiled,
that made me raise my chin to defiant
heights in response—words
so true it hurt to deny them:
*I miss him too.*

**xxvii.**

The moon was just past full
on our father's 31st birthday—

an omen—when he went to South Dakota
where women were waiting

for hunters and drunks, returned
married to a towering dark-haired

woman with a young son. It was not
in our natures to point out *her* boy

was just the age our brother
would have been. We kept silence,

let our father's story wash over us—
*finally happy*—believed in

his belief—no, he was always
casting for truth, whatever

would lift to the surface. Taught
to be good girls, we pretended

not to mind this replacement boy—
even agreed to hold his hand

crossing the street as if
nothing had changed.

**xxviii.**

September came with its flagrant
announcement of destruction,

flamboyant death-clothes. We returned
to school. Cool air bit our bare

knees, tossed our hair into frenzies.
Fourth grade was here, where math

turned suddenly incomprehensible.
I knew that everyone knew

I was minus one. Banked on
their embarrassment: who would ever

ask, *How are you now that your only
brother is dead?* To ward off even silent

pity, my chin would rise to ridiculous
heights: *I'm fine.* Distant, smiling.

They could look at me and never see
anything resembling the truth.

**xxix.**

We prayed for others, not
ourselves, special prayers for our dead

relatives, adding names as they
accrued: *Stub and Grandpa and Timmy,*

*Bud and Mildred and George.*
If they couldn't come back,

what was the point? If my mother
had known my doubt,

she would have dragged me
to confession, so I kept it

hidden—invited it. When the time
came to ask God for something

myself, I was speechless.
Figured I was born to do it

on my own. Coughed up some
excuse. Called it prayer.

# 5 : NO LEAVING

## Aristotle Said

i. *A place may be left behind by that whose place
it is.*


Aristotle fails to note the changed
nature of the place left: squat toads

hopping through grass crimp each
blade. Snakes skimming the surface

of a pool send water arcing away
in delicate swirls. We children

cut through yards and vacated
construction sites, snatched spare board

ends. We ran and fought with sticks,
tagged each other until dark, waded

the creek plucking crayfish from under
rocks before they *whooshed*

away, the water turning to dark
clouds. We left prints in muddy

driveways and on our mother's rugs.
There is no leaving—our house

keeps possession of you, hums
with your fingerprints

and laughter, even though
you were here among us, then weren't.

**ii.**  *"Down" is not any chance direction but where*
*what has weight and what is made of earth are*
*carried.*


We buried you below our sight—
laid down flowers and words

we hoped would be eternal—
our tears falling toward you, just as

when we stumbled or collapsed
onto beds, we slanted in your

direction—down—the only gestures
allowed by the God who made us

from the same material but divided us
from you—and the realms from each other.

**iii.** *For just as there can be no differentiae in*
    *nothingness, so there are none in non-being.*


Numbness: feeling of nothing—
absence of feeling? Overflow

that overwhelms
to disintegration? Soldiering

home from the funeral, bumping
shoulders as days splashed

with grief blend together. Soon
your form, holograph flashing

in rooms, lightens around
the edges, disappearing. We

strain to see. Finally, cannot feel
or sense the plumpness

of your cheeks or forearms.
Little difference whether

you left or we couldn't
keep you. Sum still

equals zero.

**iv.** *Body that travels or is let go divides the*
*medium either by its shape or by the*
*preponderance of its weight.*


Heaven must be real after all—
presence measurable

by an abstract calibration
we can't comprehend or see—

godly parting of the waters,
breath of atmosphere

riffling like a boat's wake—
no matter our ignorance.

We can call it *ether* or anything.
You're not still, that's the point.

You're making a splash
somewhere. That counts

for a lot.

**v.**   *An object moves from one place to another*
*place insofar as it is first (earlier) at the one*
*place and then (later) at the other place.*

—a paraphrase of Aristotle by Michael
Bradie and Comer Duncan


From earlier to later—usually
we call that living.

Our earlier was ease
before grief—mashed potatoes

licked from your fingers and tag
and just-combed wet hair.

Our later: space thick with
absence. Much later: we don't know

your later, how time proceeds—
if. Maybe you exist in an earlier

earlier, seeing us as we were
before you arrived, how your shape

shaped us, then seeing your own
trajectory from seed to child

to present—separate and distant
from us—as if your movement

toward God made you
indistinguishable from Him.

# 6: SHAPELESS AS THE DARK

**xxx.**

The way the wind holds its breath
before a storm—so the power of it

will be a surprise—is the way God
overcame me once. Sixteen,

exhausted by resistance, I weep
even as his storm of greeting sweeps

away my tears. I groove on the new
soundtrack for my life, scratchy

album I snug under
the turntable's arm each morning:

*We hold a treasure*
*not made of gold*

*in earthen vessels,*
*wealth untold.*

It's dizzying: my new importance.
I hold still to keep it. Later,

exhale a promise: *I'll be a nun*
*if that's what you want.*

God saw through me, prevented
my escape: I would love a man,

bear children—boys—reminder
of who's in charge, who sways

under the burden of *yes* or *no.*

**xxxi.**

This is how to bear losing
boys: Lock what is left

in memory. Tell
everyone who asks, *I have*

*two sisters. I have no*
*father.* Walk with your eyes cast

forward, in utter confidence,
until they say, *You walk like*

*a man.* Consort only with
the literal—I'll be there

means in the flesh. Expect
it. Doubt it. Believe

that wanting can be as good
as having (having always fraught

with uncertainty). Pray with
your eyes open, alert to nuances

of visitation, and greet them not
with hope, but suspicion.

**xxxii.**

Never a time I get up when
that torch doesn't tell her story:

my mother's lit cigarette
a bright arc curving

up and down, a sparkler
in winter. Later I see what

she's fashioned with the shit
you can't make up. She had to

do something with those words
he bequeathed—for comfort

or torment: *Where do you go
when you die?*

On that very day—imagine!—
calling her at work: *Can't you*

*come home for lunch?* Her quick,
tossed-off response: *You know*

*I can't come home for lunch
every day.* Most painful,

briefest pause: *I just want you
to come home today.* A heap

of meaning, shapeless as the dark.
What else could she do

but interpret it so it could
fit on a placard? She declared:

*He knew he was going to die.* Her conviction became her prayer:

*If he knew, it couldn't have been an accident*—an event

she might have prevented.

**xxxiii.**

Indian summer carves
a parenthesis, space for heat

and light to linger. Dumbly,
obeying our natures, we slow down

to admire leaves twirling on warm
breeze, their vibrant jeweled

surfaces. We accept the lie
in this respite: everything

will diminish, but we don't
have to face it. These same

brilliant leaves will brown, curl
in on themselves until

they resemble the hands
of the very old about to exit

this world and enter . . .
whatever comes next.

Everything bends toward
that possibility.

Even we wish it, sometimes.

**xxxiv.**

My sister stares at me
like I've just told her
to fuck off.

*You were there,* she says
in disbelief.
*I remember it.*

*No, I wasn't,*
I say again. *I was at the park.*
*A neighbor came to get me,*
*then I rode home by myself.*
*Afterwards.*

She shakes her head,
eyes me sadly. *You're wrong.*
*I remember it.*
*You were there.*

I am not sure which
is worse: knowing
you are in hell or believing
you are really in heaven.

**XXXV.**

There were so many who didn't know
how to kiss, who begged me with open

mouths and flailing tongues: *just fall
in.* Others who felt compelled to tell me

about the sex they'd had on overnight
shifts at the group home while

residents slept; or with the girlfriend
while the fiancée remained oblivious; or

with the drunk ex-wife after she had
passed out. I must've seemed

a priest or the screen behind which
he hid—their secrets poured out.

I became instrumental: their necessity.
Such a height from which to fall.

I never saved any of them, those boys
who were wounded to the point

of death (or dead already).

## xxxvi.

First, I chose the man—leapt
over the chasm to his foreign,

unyielding faith—then I got
to choose the name for my first

son because God and his father
were busy keeping up appearances.

They were almost mirror images:
commanding and withholding. I was not

in their field of vision. My lasting
gesture to copy myself: here

and here and here. I gave him my brother's
name—a middle name—to defy

some holy idea of fate, declare
that he would belong to me. As soon as

he was old enough, I showed him
my brother's grave. Once, he laid

a few stones on the marker, idea he got
from a book (a book I chose). Taps on

the granite so slight, they might
have been a heartbeat.

**xxxvii.**

So many ways to fall: carrying
the laundry basket—*step*—

*slip*—*thump*—on the butt—
how I fell eight months along.

Or the forward lurch, one heel
snagged in the hem of a Christmas

dress, clothes and shoes flung
outward, pregnancy preceding me

by half a step. Two out of three
times it happened. No harm

to either boy. But the abrading
of hope. Waiting to feel

movement. The stories repeated
long afterwards so the endings

couldn't suddenly change.

**xxxviii.**

When my oldest son fell down
the stairs, he was almost three—

broken arm from breaking his fall.
When my middle son fell down

the stairs at a year and a half, he did it
on purpose, to practice being big.

I found him two steps above
the landing, watched him release

the railing, throw himself forward,
feet just grazing carpet, and land flat

on his belly—then stand up to do it
again. He was undeterred, unhurt—

or pretending to be. So unlike
my brother—kin, yes—but more like

me—stubbornness that made me
shy, proud. Later, when that boy

I raised took to drink, he impersonated
my father: an ignorance of risk,

immunity to pain, refusal
to heed—and I finally saw

whom he had always resembled.

**xxxix.**

Each time one of my three boys

is about to turn four,
the age my brother fell

just short of, my childless

sister calls me. *Hi, I've been
thinking of you.* Then:

*Are you thinking about*

*him? Aren't you worried that—*
insert name of suspect boy—

*will fall?* Can't say much—

Can't say, *I am.*
Can't say, *Not until now.*

This is how I raise

boys: refuse to anticipate
death, anticipate being

a degree of welcoming.

**xl.**

His arm was in a cast from his recent fall
when he wrote the words, sitting

in church with me because he couldn't play
safely in the nursery. *God Jesus* in pencil,

huge letters. It was hard, his eyes said,
to write left-handed. I smiled down—

*my little believing boy*—even though
he was just trying to be good.

The preacher raised both arms
in the air to make a point, brought them

down on the pulpit, a stuttering
punctuation to a sentence I didn't

want to hear now that I saw how much
it pleased me to have my boy

want to please me. My arm
tightened around his shoulders,

shield to ward off this dark
passion that could lure him to God

and away from me.

**xli.**

They will devour the centers
of slices of bread and bologna,

cast the hollowed circles
to the linoleum, and you will let

them. They will grab handfuls of dirt
from plants and scatter it, refuse

to pick up toys or sit close to you
when you read, and you will let them.

They will write on the walls and later
will write papers that will make you sick

at their indifference, and laugh
when you try to help, and what choice

do you have but to let them?
They will get jobs because you

cheer them on, even buy them a car
so they can leave you more efficiently.

They will tell you, *It's your fault
I'm not doing my homework,*

will stop reading anything. They
will make you the butt of jokes

you don't understand. They will buy
you nothing for Mother's Day,

and you will always let them.

# 7: CRIES OF SUCH PITCH

**xlii.**

Two things I have learned:
Not all deaths

involve a body. The throat
of a child is too small

to swallow the whole truth.
I didn't find out until

years later. My mother
nearly kept it secret. I nearly

forgave my father everything:
not one but two affairs:

both the neighbors, wife and
husband, all together in the same

bed. One would have been
sufficient but my father never knew

when to stop. When my mother
told me, I thought stupidly, *Love*

*thy neighbor.* I remembered
the stout man who ran over

his own toes mowing the lawn,
the woman who fed me soup

when I stayed home sick.
After that, I could take in

anything: news of my father's
other fling with my sister's

godmother, what he once
whispered to my mother:

*No one else wants you.*

**xliii.**

I may have gotten this wrong:

you scribbled in a book once—
book borrowed from my teacher—
*Charlotte's Web*—
you must've been two—

and I told my first lie to the teacher:
*I lost your book.*

But our mother, who could read
the minds of dust motes, found out,
made me spend my own money
to buy my teacher a replacement book
she didn't want.

Where are you in this story?
Where the lost teacher?

I can't even remember
finding the defaced book
or recall speaking to you in anger
(you were so little—I pray
I spared you my scalding words).

My memory's slight—
petty. Our mother
may have been right.

*You should be ashamed
of yourself,*
is what she said to me.

**xliv.**

Suppose the carrots I tug
to air, beets that resist

surfacing, do not just
send showers of dirt

upward into wide
sunlight—suppose

their abrupt unearthing
unleashes cries of such

pitch the human ear
cannot detect them.

## xlv.

Not a field, a garden—
late October light.

The last melons, too young
to pick at frost, gone

to mush and seed, vines
dry as raffia. I fill

the wheelbarrow with fodder
for compost, but I can't shake

the garden's hold: my hands
tacky with sour juice and seeds.

Dirt packed under my nails
so tightly it will take days.

Weeds that thrive this late
are dug in. Their roots, sequestered

by earth, will become earth.
Next year, I will not have to

remember what I planted here.
It will all return. If I don't want

melons, I should bury this ground
under a foot of leaves.

Tamp them down. Prevent
such visitations.

**xlvi.**

So strange I want to
deny it. But no: I have seen

you, felt you: at the bottom
right corner of my bed

(shape passing through
vision) as I woke

from a dream. Your hands
on my hands on the steering wheel,

sudden and warm—not
frightening—while I waited

for the light to change.
Maybe I am becoming

my crazy great-grandmother
who once said, *Honey, sometimes*

*you just have to scream until*
*you laugh.* Each time I knew

it was you, certainty that usually
means fake. The psychic says

you forgive me for not being there
for your great event.

Who is she to know? I will keep
hoping for a next time,

even if I'm imagining all this.

**xlvii.**

I am 50, and I've never seen
the clipping from the Madison, Minnesota

newspaper—our father's birthplace.
My mother hands it to me: chatty, newsy,

a story for the living: how my brother
had fallen off a trike a few days

before the real fall. The boy
had a *lingering illness.* He's survived

by all of us. All these years
my mother has hidden the clipping

and her fury: *He was fine. Not
sick. They're saying that's why*

*he died.* All the old aunts
who may have made it up

are dead. Only my mother's anger
remains alive. No one will steal it

from her, that indignation:
it was God's story to tell. He

decided on the details. *Goddamn
it,* no one will tell her otherwise.

**xlviii.**


We go to a house of fun
to laugh at our distorted

shapes in the mirrors,
all the varying forms

curved surfaces can make of us.
Which double selves and broad

faces are most hilarious?
As for me, I am drawn like a moth

to the concave mirrors
wherein I grow smaller

than any person should be
and, depending on the angle—

though I don't understand
the physics—disappear completely.

**xlix.**

Holding onto belief
across a lifetime

is like playing Scrabble
with God who, though

he could conjure any letters
he wants, reverts

to the predictable: *always*,
he spells, *forever*, and—his

favorite—*heaven*. Using
many vowels—hoarding

them—he forces me to depend
on what he's played.

Sometimes I manage
five-letter creations—*heavy*

or *break*—or bend His rules
by rearranging His letters

instead: *sway* or *err* or *even*.
Often, out of time and luck,

I spell the simple, expected *Yes*.

1.

I am still surrounded by boys,
now men. Such a relief—

my comfort. We make a circle
in our complicated devotion

not unlike the moon snagged
in the branches of my shaggy

pine. I step outside to admire:
such luminous girth.

It floats, weighty, translucent,
beautiful, so low I could almost . . .

but that would ruin the awe
that escapes in its simplest

form, a single expelled breath—
*oh*—testament to what I love

but can never touch.

# NOTES

In xvi. "Memories are like this: beach," several lines appear from the song most famously known as "Turn! Turn! Turn!" written by Pete Seeger, which quotes Ecclesiastes 3:1–8 (KJV) in a rearranged order. Copyright © by Pete Seeger.

In xxx. "The way the wind holds its breath," four lines appear from the song/hymn referred to as "Earthen Vessels," written by John B. Foley, SJ. Copyright © 1975, 1978 by John B. Foley, SJ and New Dawn Music.

Epigraphs for "Aristotle Said" come from Chapter 5, "Aristotle on Space, Time, and Motion," of Michael Bradie and Comer Duncan's *The Evolution of the Concepts of Space and Time* (https://physics.bgsu.edu/p433/titlepage.tableofcontents.html). Epigraphs for i through iv are direct quotes from Aristotle, according to Bradie and Duncan's text. The epigraph for v is a paraphrase of Aristotle by Bradie and Duncan.

# ACKNOWLEDGMENTS

I am grateful to the editors of the following publications in which these poems first appeared:

*DMQ Review*: "Even when it appears, the truth"; "We didn't know him except"

*neat*: "Silence of aftermath:"

I am indebted to the many friends and fellow writers who devoted time and energy to providing feedback on drafts of individual poems in this book, as well as the complete manuscript as it took shape. This book would not have come to life without their generosity and talent. My heartfelt thanks to Annie Kim, Marcia Pelletiere, Kirsten Dierking, Kathy Weihe, Ann Iverson, Janet Jerve, and Marie Rickmyer.

I am grateful to the staff at CavanKerry Press for selecting this book and for the careful guidance they provided all along the way to its publication. Special thanks to Gabriel Cleveland, Managing Editor and communicator extraordinaire; Baron Wormser, whose editorial guidance helped me see new possibilities for my work; and Joy Arbor, whose keen copyediting eye brought the book to its final polished form. I felt the support of a full team all along the way, a rare and rewarding experience.

# CAVANKERRY'S MISSION

A not-for-profit literary press serving art and community, Cavan-Kerry is committed to expanding the reach of poetry and other fine literature to a general readership by publishing works that explore the emotional and psychological landscapes of everyday life, and to bringing that art to the underserved where they live, work, and receive services.

# OTHER BOOKS IN THE EMERGING VOICES SERIES

*Boy* was typeset in Arno Pro, which was created by Robert Slimbach at Adobe. The name refers to the river that runs through Florence, Italy.